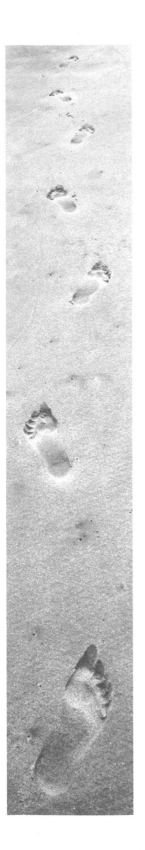

Finding
God
in Prayer
A Backpack
Journal
for Teens

Gary Giombi

Pflaum Publishing Group
Dayton, OH 45439
1-800-543-4383
www.Pflaum.com

Cover and interior design: Ellen Wright
Cover photos: W.P. Wittman Photography Ltd.
Editor: Karen Cannizzo

Fourth Printing: 2008

Pflaum Publishing Group
2621 Dryden Road, Suite 300
Dayton, OH 45439
800-543-4383
www.pflaum.com

ISBN 978-0-89837-196-3

The Journey of Prayer

You are now beginning a guidebook for an important journey, the journey of prayer. What do you need to bring along with you? Bring along relaxation. Although your journey requires hard work, it also requires time to relax. Let your body relax so that you have the energy you need for the long miles ahead. Let your mind relax by putting away your preconceptions and prejudices. Bring along several important attitudes: openness to try any path and see where it leads, endurance to exert yourself climbing mountains, and courage to see the truth wherever you may find it.

What is the destination of your journey, the center of your labyrinth? Don't just say "God." Begin by saying that it is a journey to your best and truest self. It is a voyage to the depths of your soul, and it is there that you will find God.

Journaling and Prayer

A good way to reflect on your life and your relationship with God is to keep a prayer journal. A journal contains your reflections and feelings about what has been occurring on your life-journey. It can be a collection of "letters to God" about your life.

Keeping a journal can be a form of prayer. Not only can you write about how you find God in your life, but also as you are writing, you will experience the continuing presence of God. The writing itself will become a prayer. When you use your journal to record your prayers, you will find that they pray themselves again as you write or reread them.

Write. **Pray.** **Do.**

How to Use This Book

You do not have to do the prayers and activities in this book in the order they are given, although it would be better to do so. You can also skip any that do not seem meaningful to you, although you may profit from an experience to which you were not at first attracted.

You will notice that the prayers and activities are marked with stepping stones. There are more than 200. On the inside of the front cover of the book is a labyrinth like the one above, but with 144 stepping stones leading to its center, a number representing total fulfillment in the Scriptures. After you complete any prayer or exercise, check off the stone(s). Then go to the labyrinth and check off or fill in the same number of stones. Begin at the bottom of the labyrinth and move toward the center. By the time you reach the center, you will have found something valuable there. You will have gotten to know yourself and God better. Then walk and pray your way back along the same path.

Take five to ten minutes for each prayer or activity. Unless instructed otherwise, go to a quiet place to pray. Write this prayer journal in such a way that it will be understandable to you and still have something to say to you ten years after you have completed it. Be sure to keep it in a safe and special place where people will not get at it. You might even consider putting a "pen name" into the book in case someone else should find and read it.

Along with a variety of prayers, this book suggests activities for you to try, including some in which you will search on the Internet. You will not be given any URLs, but your favorite search engine will help you. The book also gives you an opportunity to think about and put into practice the Beatitudes and the works of mercy. You will learn about the seven capital sins, which are called "capital" because they can lead to other sins. You will be encouraged to avoid the capital sins as orientations that can mess up your life.

Reflecting on Your Relationship with God

Since this book will help you develop a better relationship with your Friend, God, begin the prayerful journaling process by thinking about friendship.

○ **Write.** Briefly describe your relationship with your best friend. Then check off the stepping stone here and the first stone at the entrance to the labyrinth on the inside of the front cover.

○ **Pray.** Pray for your best friend. When you're done, check off the stone here and the next stone on the labyrinth.

○ **Write.** A one-sentence prayer for your friend. Check off this stone and the next stone on the labyrinth.

○ **Write.** Describe your current relationship with your Friend, God. Then check off this stone and the next stone on the labyrinth. (This is the last time you will get this reminder.)

Becoming a More Prayerful Person

You can improve your relationship with God and get more in touch with yourself by becoming a more reflective and prayerful person. This book will help you on this journey. But you will have to provide the commitment and effort. This will take self-discipline. You will need to take the time and the concentration to work through the book. And it will be work. Nothing valuable, except God's love, which is always freely and unconditionally given, comes without hard work. It takes work for us to open ourselves to God's presence and love. To help you be faithful to this journey, you can enter your extra prayers—for instance, prayers before bed—into the Prayer Log on the inside back cover of this book.

 Pray. Just pray as you usually do, when you are not in church.

Write. What do you do when you pray? What happens in your mind, heart, and body?

Prayer Can Help You

- Reach your potential and develop your capabilities
- Become a better and more loving person
- Improve your attitudes, become calmer, more patient and loving
- Grow from whatever happens in your life
- Deepen your relationship with the Person who loves you the most, God
- Recognize that God walks with you through your life
- Become more aware of and concerned about the needs of others
- Appreciate all the good things God has given you
- Develop compassion for what most of the world's people suffer
- Bear your own sorrows

Jesus told us that if we ask God for any good thing in Jesus' name, God will give it to us. Prayer is that asking. Prayer is opening yourself to receive what God is offering you. Through prayer you can funnel God's power and energy into the world.

Pray. To benefit from this prayer journal.

Speaking and Listening to God

Prayer is a conversation. We speak to God and God speaks to us. This is a main insight of the Christian, Jewish, and Islamic faiths—God speaks to us human beings. One special Word that God speaks reveals to us what God is like. And that Word is Jesus, the Word of God made flesh.

Write. Who is Jesus for you? The Son of God? A healer? Just a person you admire? Someone you don't think much about?

Pray. *Letter to Jesus*
God sometimes speaks, but God always listens. It may seem difficult to have a prayer conversation with God or Jesus because they don't seem to talk. Sometimes we have to listen not just for words or ideas, but also for feelings. Write a short prayerful letter to Jesus telling him about your life. Pay attention to your feelings as you write.

Do. Be a communicative Jesus to someone. Send someone who needs support an encouraging note or e-mail, but sign it J.C. This follows what St. Paul writes, "…it is no longer I who live, but it is Christ who lives in me." (Galatians 2:20)

Speaking and Living the Truth

Jesus said, "I am the way, and the truth, and the life." (John 14:6) If we are to be prayerful people, we need lips that do not lie and ears that have not been bewitched by falsehoods. Otherwise in our prayer we will not speak clearly or listen well.

Write. How well do you speak the truth and live the truth?

Pray. *Cloud Memories*
Read this guided fantasy prayer a few times before you pray it. Take a minute to calm your mind and relax your body. Imagine you are sitting on a beach on a beautiful spring day. Jesus is sitting next to you. You are watching big, billowy clouds float across the sky. They seem to form shapes that remind you of some of the important events from your life. Think of events from your early childhood, grade school years, vacations, home life, high school years, this last year, the last few weeks, and so on. Really put yourself back into the events and talk to Jesus about what you see.

In the clouds on the page facing this one, describe some of the important events of your life. Also write in each cloud what Jesus might say about the event.

Do. Contact someone whom you have not seen for a while who was in one of your positive memories.

Do. Surf the web or skim a newspaper looking for examples of lies. On the next occasion when you are tempted to lie, be brave and tell the truth.

Write. Describe how your prayers and activities went and what you learned from them. Then write a one-sentence prayer that sums up your experiences with prayers and activities on this page and the next page.

Cloud Memories

Talking with Jesus

Write. In each of these Scripture passages, Jesus is speaking to you. Think about what he is saying and then write a short response. What would you say to Jesus?

"Do not be afraid." (John 6:20)

"I came that they may have life, and have it abundantly." (John 10:10)

"For I have come to call not the righteous but sinners." (Matthew 9:13)

"All these things [which you need] will be given you as well." (Matthew 6:33)

Write. *Reverse Prayer*
Imagine you are Jesus and Jesus is you. Write some things that you could say as Jesus to encourage a teenager living in today's world.

Pray. Talk to Jesus about what you have written.

Walking with Jesus

Do. Find the "Footprints in the Sand" prayer on the Internet and print or purchase a copy for your room. Or use the copy on page 48 of this journal.

Pray. *Jesus Supports You*
Take a minute to calm your mind and relax your body. Deep breathing can help. Go back to the prayer in which you watched clouds with Jesus on a beach (page 8). Recall some of the more difficult times of your life and imagine Jesus supporting you as you walked through them. Read the "Footprints in the Sand" prayer slowly and talk to Jesus about it. Pay attention to your feelings.

Write. Describe a time in your life when Jesus/God has carried you and a time when you have helped carry someone who was burdened.

Write. Describe how your prayers and activities went and what you learned from them.

Practicing Humility and Mercy

Pride is the one of the seven capital sins, which are called "capital" because they can lead to other sins. Pride causes us to think that we are better than others. Even if we are better than others at doing some particular thing, we can never judge that we are better persons than others. When people are too proud, they do not even want to talk to anyone "beneath" them. But remember that Jesus "did not regard equality with God as something to be exploited, but emptied himself, taking the form of a slave." (Philippians 2:6-7) If we are too proud, it is difficult to be prayerful.

The Beatitude, "Blessed are the merciful, for they will receive mercy" (Matthew 5: 7), is the opposite of pride. The merciful person considers others to be equals and tries to raise others up when circumstances bring them down.

Pray. Humility, the opposite of pride, means to be down to earth and see others as your equals. Think of some of the saints who were humble, such as Peter who wept when he denied Jesus. Pray to be a person of humility, not of pride. Think of persons who have been merciful, perhaps to you, and pray to be a person of mercy yourself.

Write. Describe your prayer, feelings as well as words and thoughts.

Do. Be merciful and humble like Jesus by talking to an "outcast" at school. Think before you decide to do this because it may lay further demands upon you.

Do. The work of mercy, "Counsel the doubtful." Be like Jesus by helping or encouraging someone with his or her homework. But don't just provide the answers!

Write. Describe how your prayers and activities went and what you learned from them. Then write a one-sentence prayer that sums up your experience doing this page.

Describing God

"O give thanks to the Lord, for he is good; for his steadfast love endures forever." (Psalm 107:1) When we speak, even to God, one of the best things we can say is "Thank you." But who is this God we thank? Jesus is perhaps our best image of God. Another image is the loving *Abba* (Daddy), the name that Jesus called God.

 Write. What are some of your images or descriptions of God?

Pray. *Abba*
Take a minute to calm your mind and relax your body. In this litany repetition prayer, mentally repeat the word *Abba*. As you slowly inhale, pray the sound "Ah." As you slowly exhale, pray the sound "Bah." As you raise your mind and heart to God, repeat *Abba* over and over with your breathing.

Write. How did this prayer affect your mind, heart, and body?

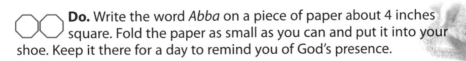

Do. Write the word *Abba* on a piece of paper about 4 inches square. Fold the paper as small as you can and put it into your shoe. Keep it there for a day to remind you of God's presence.

Write. Describe how your prayers and activities went and what you learned from them. Then write a one-sentence prayer that sums up your experience doing this page.

Developing an Attitude of Gratitude

Write. We can be grateful to God for all the good things in our lives. List 50 things you like to do. Force yourself to actually list 50.

50 Things I like to Do

1. _____
2. _____
3. _____
4. _____
5. _____
6. _____
7. _____
8. _____
9. _____
10. _____
11. _____
12. _____
13. _____
14. _____
15. _____
16. _____
17. _____
18. _____
19. _____
20. _____
21. _____
22. _____
23. _____
24. _____
25. _____

26. _____
27. _____
28. _____
29. _____
30. _____
31. _____
32. _____
33. _____
34. _____
35. _____
36. _____
37. _____
38. _____
39. _____
40. _____
41. _____
42. _____
43. _____
44. _____
45. _____
46. _____
47. _____
48. _____
49. _____
50. _____

Now go back and put a "$" after any activities that cost money at the time you do them. Put an "A" after things that you tend to do alone. Put a "P" after any that your parents also enjoy doing. Put an "R" after any that you have done recently, within the last six months. Put a "B" after any that are not good for you.

Pray. Talk to God about what you learned about yourself from this activity.

Praying Your Personal Version of the Lord's Prayer

Pray. Adapt the Lord's Prayer by changing some words so it meets your special situation today. The words in the parentheses are the original words that you can change in your prayer. For instance, if you are on a team, you might begin the prayer, "Our Coach, who art encouraging us…." If you are having trouble with school, you might pray, "Our Teacher, who art in the classroom…."

Our (Father) _____, who art (in heaven) _____,

(hallowed) _____ be thy (name) _____;

thy (kingdom) _____ (come) _____;

thy (will) _____ (be done) _____

on (earth) _____ as it is in (heaven) _____.

Give us this day our (daily bread) _____;

and forgive (us our trespasses) _____

as (we forgive those who trespass against us) _____;

and lead us not (into temptation) _____,

but deliver us from (evil) _____. Amen.

Write. Describe how your prayerful activity went and what you learned from it.

Reflecting on Family and Friends

Although some family situations are far from perfect, we do owe a lot to our family and relatives. We have received some of their good qualities, either through nature (genes) or nurture (influence).

Do. Create a family tree with your immediate family, grandparents, aunts, uncles, and (perhaps) cousins. These names can be written on the branches of the tree. On the trunk you can write the initials of your friends. For each family member or friend, write some good quality of his or hers that you also have.

Do. Phone a relative or friend and thank this person for something good he or she has done for you.

Write. A short prayer of gratitude for all the good people in your life and good qualities that you have.

Finding God in Friends and Family

○ **Pray.** Some of your friends and family members may be good images of God for you. Go back and look again at your family tree. Select some of the people named there and say short prayers for them.

○ **Pray.** *Finding God at Your School*
You might want to read this next prayer over a few times before praying it. Take a minute to calm your mind and relax your body. For the next few minutes, in your imagination, walk through your school looking for God. Please put away any preconceptions about where you might find God or what God might look like. Use all your senses. Feel the roughness of the walls; smell the aroma of fresh paint in the maintenance shop; taste the food in the cafeteria; and so on. Look all over for God, even in unexpected places. If you need assistance, do not hesitate to imagine someone to ask for help in finding God. When you find God, imagine yourself talking to God and then listening for what God may say in reply. If you do not seem to find God, just be aware of whatever you see in your imagination. Now take some time to search for God.

○ **Write.** *Describe Your Looking for God*
This prayer can tell you much about what you think about God, how you relate to God, and where you find God in your life. If you do not find God at all, it may indicate that God is missing from your life right now, or that God is so present that you don't have to see God, or that it just will take a few times for this guided fantasy prayer to work. If you found only people at your school, but not God, perhaps you have actually found God because God is especially present in people. Describe where you found God.

○○ **Do.** Write a thank-you note to a friend or fellow student in whom you have seen God. Or, go to where you found God and put up a small paper heart.

○ **Pray.** You can also pray this guided fantasy by looking for God in your home, at your work, in your city, or wherever you wish to look.

Reflecting on Other VIPs

Write. You've been reflecting on your friends and family. Who else has been influential in your life? List six people and how they have influenced you.

1. _____   2. _____

   _____   _____

3. _____   4. _____

   _____   _____

5. _____   6. _____

   _____   _____

Do. Sometimes people are influenced by athletes and musicians. The Book of Psalms in the Bible has song/poems that Jews and Christians have prayed for over 2500 years. Go to the Internet and download a copy of Psalm 23, "The Lord is My Shepherd." You can also find a copy on page 47.

Pray. Find the "Interview with God" website and prayerfully view the video version of Psalm 23.

Pray. Take a copy of Psalm 23, either from your Bible or from the web, and pray it as *Lectio Divina*. This means to read it slowly and prayerfully one line at a time. After each phrase or line, also listen for what God may want to tell you.

Write. Describe how your prayers and activities went and what you learned from them. Then write a one-sentence prayer that sums up your experience doing this page.

Always Wanting More

The capital sin of gluttony is worse than just eating or drinking too much. It is the opposite of gratitude. It means not appreciating what you have and always wanting more. According to Buddhists, the craving desires that fuel gluttony are the source of the suffering in our life. According to Jesus in the Beatitudes, we should "hunger and thirst for righteousness [justice]" (Matthew 5:6), rather than for money and possessions.

Write. List some times in your life when not having what you wanted made you unhappy. How would Jesus' or Buddha's advice have helped you?

Pray. Try a gentle fast of eating a little less for meals and not eating between meals, and see what that is like. Some people suggest that not eating or drinking (other than water) between supper and bedtime is a healthy practice. When you feel hungry, let that remind you to pray in gratitude for what you have and for the many others who have less than you.

Do. Over a period of a few days, notice how often and how much you eat, even candy.

Do. Read the corporal works of mercy on page 47 of this journal. Try one of the corporal works of mercy to help you focus on others rather than on yourself.

Write. Describe how your prayers and activities went and what you learned from them. Then write a one-sentence prayer that sums up your experience doing this page.

Expressing Sorrow, Asking for Forgiveness

Have mercy on me, O God,
according to your steadfast love;
according to your abundant mercy
blot out my transgressions.

Psalm 51:1

In your relationship with God, just as in any other relationship, there are times to express sorrow and ask for forgiveness. A relationship that lacks these expressions will not grow.

Write. Describe some of the suffering you have caused others and some that you yourself have experienced.

Pray. *Kyrie Eleison*

Repeating the prayer *Kyrie Eleison* (Greek for "Lord, have mercy"), in rhythm with your breathing is a wonderful prayer, both to ask forgiveness for wrongs you have done and also to ask for help for people who are suffering. Mentally pray *Key ree ay,* or "Lord," as you inhale; *ay lay ee sone,* or "have mercy," as you exhale. If you remember one and like it, use the melody of a hymn or a response from Mass for these words.

Do. If you no longer pray to God before bed, try returning to that practice. As part of this prayer, remember the good things of the day and thank God. Remember the times you fell short of the mark and ask God's forgiveness.

Do. Experience receiving forgiveness. Go to someone you have hurt and ask for forgiveness. Or go to the Sacrament of Reconciliation. Or, during the first part of the Mass—the Penitential Rite—ask God for forgiveness.

Write. A one-sentence prayer that sums up your experience doing this page.

Forgiving and Not Judging

Jesus told us not to judge others (Luke 6:37), and to forgive them seventy-seven times—always (Matthew 18:22).

Write. Describe a time when:
• You were judged wrongly

• You judged wrongly

• You were forgiven

• You forgave

Pray. *Prayer of Sorrow and Recommitment*
O God, I am sorry with all my heart for all my sins, for all the times I have hurt other people, myself, and You. I am sorry for these sins because of the pain they have caused others, and the pain they have caused me in my life and will cause me in my death. I am sorry that they have hurt You, my God, who is present in all people, especially the suffering. I will really try not to do these hurtful things again, to commit these unloving sins again. Please help me.

Write. Describe how your prayers and activities went and what you learned from them. Then write a one-sentence prayer that sums up your experience doing this page.

Getting to Know Yourself and Others

Write. You may use abbreviations so that no one will know what you have written.

Six things you dislike about other people

1.

2.

3.

4.

5.

6.

Six things you dislike about yourself

1.

2.

3.

4.

5.

6.

Six things you like about other people

1.

2.

3.

4.

5.

6.

Six things you like about yourself

1.

2.

3.

4.

5.

6.

Now compare the lists and connect any items that are on both "like" lists or on both "dislike" lists. Did you find many things you dislike in other people you also dislike in yourself? Did you find that many things you like in other people you also like in yourself? If you did, then you have discovered the principle of "projection," that what we are strongly aware of in others is also in us, at least as a tendency. If you did not find connections, then you need to get to know yourself better because you really have in yourself what you like or dislike in others.

Pray. About this activity.

Needing and Wanting to Be Healed

○ **Pray.** Open your Bible to John 5:1-9. Imagine you are the man that Jesus cures. Slowly and prayerfully read the passage. As you read consider the following:

> Imagine how hopeless and frustrated you would feel if you had been ill for 38 years.
>
> Hear Jesus asking you if you want to be healed. In real life, you actually do not have paralyzed legs, but you do need to be healed nonetheless. Take a minute to get in touch with some of the areas of your life that may need healing.
>
> Jesus is ready to heal you, but you can neither ask to be healed nor can you admit that you need healing. To be healed would be very frightening. It would mean starting a whole new way of life after you had grown comfortable with your limited one. In real life, if you were no longer lazy, you would have to work harder. If you no longer had a cynical tongue, you would not have the fun of cutting people down, and so on.
>
> Jesus knows that in your heart of hearts, underneath all the fear and cowardice, you really do want to be healed. And so he heals you.

○ **Write.** How would it feel to be cured of 38 years of paralysis? How would it feel to be cured of your own ailments or personal problems? What would your new life be like?

○ **Write.** A prayer asking Jesus for healing.

Healing of Memories

The capital sin of anger means being hardhearted and not able to forgive. In his Beatitude Jesus asks us to be brokenhearted, not hardhearted: "Blessed are those who mourn, for they will be comforted." (Matthew 5:4)

When something bad happens to us, it can hurt us twice—at the time that it actually occurs and so long as the memory of it festers inside of us. Begin this prayer by deciding upon an event in which someone hurt you, or one in which you blame God for something, like someone's death. If you have suffered physical or sexual abuse in your life, it might be better not to use that experience for this prayer until you have dealt with it in therapy sessions with a trained counselor.

Pray. *Healing of Memories*
After relaxing, re-create the painful event in your imagination. Replay what happened. Now put yourself in the shoes of the person who hurt you. Try to see the event from his or her perspective. Try to experience how the person, given his or her background, was doing the best the person could do in these circumstances. Now try to forgive him or her. If you cannot authentically forgive the person yet, then pray to God for help to be able to someday forgive him or her. Now pray for the person who hurt you.

Write. What are the initials of the person who hurt you? What was the event? Were you able to see the event from that person's perspective? Were you able to at least partially forgive the person?

Do. The spiritual work of mercy, "Forgive all injuries," by forgiving yourself.

Do. Actually go to someone who has injured you and forgive him or her.

Write. A one-sentence prayer that sums up your experience doing this page.

Taking Our Fears to God

The heavens are telling the glory of God;
and the firmament proclaims his handiwork.
Psalm 19:1

Our loving heart prompts us to praise our friends, which means to acknowledge their goodness and speak good things about them. The Holy Spirit prompts us to praise our Friend, God. The Sacrament of Confirmation opens us to a deeper share in the Gifts of the Spirit, one of them being a sense of awe toward God.

Write. Jot down a few fears (of people, certain events, challenging goals, and so on) that sometimes bother you. Then write a one- or two-sentence prayer of praise to and confidence in God who will lead you through the valley of your fears. Remember the words of Jesus when he promised the Holy Spirit to the Apostles, "Peace be with you." (Luke 24:36-38)

Pray. Music has a way of calming our fears. Find a piece of music (religious, classical, or contemporary) that usually lifts your spirits. Listen to it as you prayerfully take your fears to God.

Do. Knowing that God's Holy Spirit will be with you, face down one of your fears. For instance, tell the truth when you want to lie, reach out to someone you do not know, do something or take a position that is not a popular one, and so on.

Write. Describe how your prayers and activities went and what you learned from them. Then write a one-sentence prayer that sums up your experience doing this page.

Experiencing God's Spirit and Light

"Do you not know that you are God's temple and that God's Spirit dwells in you?" (1 Corinthians 3:16) We are children of God, filled with the light of God and the life of the Spirit. When we pray to God, we do not have to worry about what to say. All we have to do is be there and the Spirit will pray through us.

Write. Describe an experience of God's presence that you had. It might be in nature, in another person, in a time of suffering or doubt.

Pray. Become a being of God's light. You might have a serious friend read this to you. Let your body begin to relax. Breathe just a little more deeply and slowly. Let your mind relax by letting go of any troublesome thoughts. Try to visualize God's presence as light within you in your heart.

Jesus said that he was the Light of the World. God began creation by saying, "Let there be light." Hear those words spoken to you and feel the light of God's Spirit fill your heart. That light is so intense that it cannot just remain in your heart. It begins spreading throughout your whole body, transforming your earthly body into a body of light.

First your chest, shoulders, and back are filled with the radiance of your heart and are transformed into light. They become completely relaxed. You no longer have a chest and shoulders; they are light. You feel the atoms of your arms speeding up as their electrons absorb the energy. Slowly your arms and then your hands change from flesh to light. No more arms or hands, only light. The light continues to move up through your neck and into your head. Feel your face begin to grow radiant. Now even the top of your head has become light.

Then the light from your heart begins to flow into your abdomen and lower back. They are filled with light and are changed into light. Your legs start to radiate. They begin giving off a red glow and then white light. Your feet are now filled with the light flow all the way down to your toes. You can feel them slowly turning into light. Your whole body has been transformed into a body of light. You are filled with the Holy Spirit.

Relax your thoughts by letting them turn into light. Now let the light dissolve all of your cares and worries and plans until your thoughts become just pure light. No more thoughts, only light. Relax as you experience God's Spirit and light filling your body.

 Do. Think of one action that you will take to let God's light shine through you to light other people's lives.

Draw. Fill in and around the figure below with symbols and bright colors that describe your prayer and illustrate God's Spirit and light present within you.

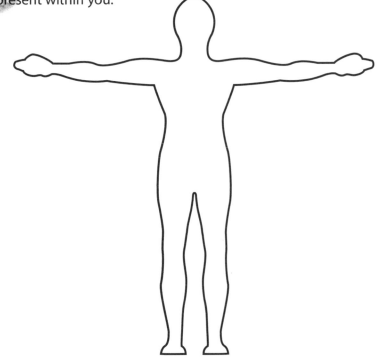

Do. Make a mini-pilgrimage. Go out and find God's presence in some special "religious" place. It might be a place of public prayer like a church, monastery, shrine, cemetery, or grotto. Or it might be a special calming place in your city or neighborhood.

Write. Describe how your prayers and activities went and what you learned from them. Then write a one-sentence prayer that sums up your experience doing this page and the previous page.

Praying to the Holy Spirit

Besides enjoying the Holy Spirit's help, we can also pray to the Spirit. We can imagine the Holy Spirit as fire, wind, electrical energy, or the calm life-giving Spirit of nature. The Bible sometimes even portrays the Holy Spirit as feminine Wisdom with a house of seven columns or gifts (Proverbs 9:1).

Pray. As you do the following activities.

Do. Find a symbolic picture of the Holy Spirit for your room or your computer's screen saver, one that touches something in your heart and spirit. Draw or describe it below.

Do. Take a walk and find the presence of God in nature.

Do. Walk through your school and see people as presences of God's Spirit.

Write. Describe how your prayers and activities went and what you learned from them. Then write a one-sentence prayer that sums up your experience doing this page.

Praising God

The capital sin of envy often results in the inability to praise people and in actually cutting them down. It is impossible to praise God while we envy other people. Jesus' Beatitude, "Blessed are the meek, for they will inherit the earth" (Matthew 5:5), reminds us to avoid the arrogance that an overly proud person may have.

○ **Write.** The initials of some people you envy and a few words describing what you envy about them.

○○ **Do.** Make an opportunity to honestly say something good about one of the people you envy.

○○ **Do.** The spiritual work of mercy, "Instruct the ignorant," by sharing your faith with someone.

○ **Write.** Describe how your prayers and activities went and what you learned from them. Then write a one-sentence prayer that sums up your experience doing this page.

Bringing Our Needs to God

Jesus said, "Ask, and it will be given you." (Matthew 7:7) This should encourage us to bring God all our needs, knowing that God answers all prayers, but only in the way that will help us most—which might not be the way we expect.

◯ **Write.** Make a list of living people you want to pray for.

◯ **Pray.** For people on your list, asking God to give them what they need most.

◯◯ **Do.** Get the main news section of a current newspaper and circle all the headlines that have to do with suffering.

◯◯ **Write.** Make a list of ten bad things that are happening that need our prayers.

1.

2.

3.

4.

5.

6.

7.

8.

9.

10.

Pray. *Prayer of Compassion*

Picture in your mind a person who has suffered a lot. It can be someone you actually know; for instance, one of your friends who has a horrible family situation, someone with an alcohol or drug problem, or someone who is doing very poorly with studies or a job. Or it can be suffering people whom you do not actually know personally; for instance, someone seriously ill in a hospital, a homeless person in your city, or a lonely person in a nursing home.

Now try to imagine that you are this person. Give the person a name if you don't know his or her name. Try to picture what a day in that person's life would be like. What is it like getting up in the morning? How do you feel about facing a new day? What is breakfast like? What happens to you in the morning? What do you do for lunch? What is the afternoon like? What happens at suppertime? What is evening like? How do you feel when it is time to go to bed?

Write. Write and pray the prayer you, as the person you are imagining, say before you sleep.

Pray. *The Jesus Prayer*

You can pray by just mentally saying the word *Jesus* as you inhale and *mercy* as you exhale. Go back and read each person or item on the two lists you made on the previous page. After each, pray "Jesus, mercy" with your breathing.

Do. Write a prayer petition and take it to church. Put it on the parish prayer board if you have one, or drop it into the collection basket. Another option is to find a "prayer requests" website on the Internet and leave it there.

Write. Describe how your prayers and activities went and what you learned from them. Then write a one-sentence prayer that sums up your experience doing this page and the previous page.

Getting in Touch with Your Life

Write. What is most important for you in your life right now, this week, not in the future?

Pray. St. Augustine once opened his Bible at random and found that it opened to a passage that gave him excellent advice for his life. Scripture can do the same for you. Read the following through to the end to get a sense of what you will be doing. Then read and follow the directions item by item.

Relax. Get in touch with your life, with what is important for you right now. Close your eyes.

Open your Bible at random. Put your finger down. Read a sentence or a few verses. Listen to it without thinking. Then think about it. Then pray over it.

If the verse you happened to pick is a list—for example, a genealogy of names—read it quickly to see whether it is meaningful. If it is not, pick again. If the passage you picked seems too strict—like cut off your hand if it is an occasion of sin to you—do not follow the advice.

Write. Describe how the Bible activity went and what you learned from it.

Write. Make a list of goals for your life under these three headings.

Within a Year   **In Ten Years**   **Before I Die**

Pray. *Three Caverns of Wisdom*

Let your body relax slowly, part by part. Then imagine yourself entering and exploring the cave of wisdom. After a while, you discover that the cave branches off into three caverns. Each one has a sign at its opening. Try to see the three signs. What is written on each sign? If you cannot make out the writing, just look down the caverns, get a feel for them, and in that way decide which one you will walk down. Each cavern has some special wisdom for you. Now take some time to explore. After a while, return to the main part of the cave. Now retrace your steps to the entrance of the cave. Step outside and return to normal reality.

Write. Fill in the signs in the illustration. Then describe what you found in the cave and what wisdom it offered you.

Pray. Talk to God about the cave experience. Ask the Holy Spirit to be the wisdom in your life.

Knowing Who We Are

Before we can know what to ask God for, we must know who we are. This *mandala*, circular prayer design, is based on a Native American medicine shield. Think of symbols for each of your personal qualities described below.

Draw.

1. In the north/winter (top) quadrant, draw something about yourself that still sleeps within you.

2. In the east/spring (right) quadrant, draw something about yourself that is just beginning in you.

3. In the south/summer (bottom) quadrant, draw something about yourself that is strong in you now.

4. In the winter/autumn (left) quadrant, draw something about yourself that is dying in you.

Write. A one-sentence prayer that sums up your experience doing this page and the previous page.

Wanting Versus Needing

The capital sin of covetousness is wanting good things only for yourself, perhaps even asking God only for things for yourself. This is very different from Jesus' Beatitude, "Blessed are the poor in spirit, for theirs is the kingdom of heaven." (Matthew 5:3)

Write. Complete these two wish lists.

Things I Want	Things I Really Need (but don't have)

Write. Compare the lists with each other and with what a very poor person might have written.

Pray. Ask God for the things you really need. Thank God that (hopefully) there are few of them.

Pray. One of the spiritual works of mercy asks us to pray for the living and the dead. Take a minute to remember friends and family who have died.

Do. Think of deceased persons whom you love and respect. As a way to keep them in mind, write one or two of these names on your upper arm where only you will see it.

Listening for God's Voice

"Be still, and know that I am God!" (Psalm 46:10) In any relationship, even our prayer relationship with God, listening is as important as speaking. These next few pages will help you hear God's voice, "a tiny whispering sound." (I Kings 19:12)

Write. Go to a quiet place where you can be alone. Write down all the sounds you hear.

Prayer Prelude. *Breathing Awareness*
The Holy Spirit is the breath of God, so take a few minutes to be aware of your breathing. You do not have to breathe deeply or to breathe in any other special way. Just breathe normally. Mentally follow the flow of the air as it enters your body, settles into your lungs, and then leaves your body. You do not have to think about your breathing, just be aware of it. Breathing exercises help you to quiet your body and mind so you can listen for God.

Write. Describe this experience. How did it relax your body and help center your mind?

Prayer Prelude. *Slow Breathing*
Gradually slow down your breathing by slowing the time you take to inhale and the time you take to exhale. Do not hold your breath or hold your lungs empty. Breathe only as slowly as you comfortably can. Be aware only of your breathing as you breathe more and more slowly. Keep slowing down your breathing as long as you comfortably can, but not slower than four times per minute.

Write. Describe this experience. How did it relax your body and help center your mind?

Deciding What's Valuable

Breathing teaches us how to let go. It is easy to feel uncomfortable if we hold our breath. But in life it is hard to let go. We want to hang on to things. And yet everything around us passes in and out of our lives like the air we breath passes through our body.

Do. Make a list below of ten items (persons, things, relationships, and so on) that you would not want to lose. Then take ten small pieces of paper and write one item on each. Decide which item you would give up if you had to lose one of them. Then rip up that piece of paper. Put the number "1" after that item on your list below. Now determine another item to give up and rip up its piece of paper. Put a number "2" after the item on the list. Keep doing this until only one item is left, the most valuable for you. Give it the number "10."

*

*

*

*

*

*

*

*

*

*

Pray. Talk to God about this letting-go exercise.

Write. About the exercise and your prayer.

Experiencing God's Presence

Pray. *Listening for God's Presence*
Lie on your back on the floor. Put a pillow under your knees so that they are bent. Breathe a bit more slowly and deeply. As you breathe, listen for whatever your deepest self or God's Spirit within you may wish to communicate to you. You don't have to speak—just be open to experiencing God's presence within you. Remember to relax your body and gently try to keep wandering thoughts out of your mind, except the feeling of God's presence.

Write. Describe this experience.

God speaks to you not just through the holy Bible. God also speaks to you through the scripture of your life. Every event in your life has a message to you from God. Every person who enters your life is a messenger, an angel from God.

Write. Think for a while about the scripture of your life. What has life taught you? What has God taught you through your life?

Living in the Present Moment

Prayer Prelude. *Watching Your Thoughts*
If you take the time to become aware of what thoughts are capturing your mind, you can learn a lot about yourself.

Imagine that your mind is a television set that you are watching, but you do not become involved in what is happening on the screen. To give you something to do while waiting for thoughts to pop into the television of your mind, just listen to all the sounds you can hear around you, but do not think about them. Then, as you become aware of your mind thinking about something, put a label on the thought and wait for the next thought to take over your mind. Some possible labels could be thoughts about the past, the future, family, school, your true love, worries, fears, and so on. Once you have noticed and labeled the thought, stop thinking it and go back to the listening until another thought takes over.

Write. Jot down some of the things that passed through your mind. What does that tell you about yourself?

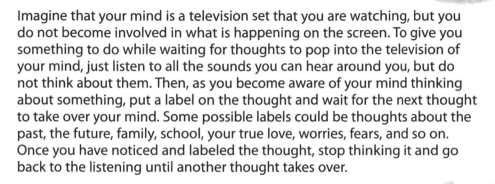

Mindfulness is living in the here and now, the present moment. Often people do not live in the here because their minds are a million miles away from where their bodies are. Nor do they live in the now. They live in the past by letting their minds be full of memories instead of attending to what is going on right now. Or, they live in the future by planning and worrying instead of experiencing what is going on around them right now. If you miss the present, you are not really alive.

Do. *Doing What You Are Doing*
Take some activity; for example, washing the dishes or mowing the lawn. Try to do it with full mindfulness; that is, just do it with full awareness and do nothing else at the same time, not even to listen to music. Or take a small piece of food and chew it 50 times. Really experience how it feels and tastes as you chew it.

Write. Describe your experience.

Challenging Our Laziness

The capital sin of sloth—laziness—is an example of taking listening too far, just being there but doing nothing. Many distractions in our life can also encourage laziness—just sitting around playing video games, watching TV, or listening to music. Jesus' Beatitude, "Blessed are the peacemakers, for they will be called children of God" (Matthew 5:9), gives us a challenge to our laziness—build peace in our world, our schools, our families, and our own hearts.

Write. What are some ways that you could be a peacemaker?

Pray. For peace and to become a peacemaker.

Do. One of the spiritual works of mercy, "Bear wrongs patiently." This is also a way of being a peacemaker, but it does not mean ignoring injustice. It means changing a situation through suffering love and nonviolent resistance rather than through violence. Mahatma Gandhi's life is a good example of this. Do an Internet search to learn more about this proponent of nonviolence.

Write. How could nonviolence help you or your school?

Do. Take some extra time to listen to God by celebrating a Sabbath. Try taking one weekend day, or at least part of the day, and not only go to church, but also refrain from shopping, going out, using electronic or electrical devices, and so on. Use the saved time to do something positive for your family.

Write. Describe your Sabbath experience.

Praying to Mary

Did you ever want something from your parents, but were afraid to ask? Perhaps you got one of your siblings to put in a good word for you to Mom or Dad. This also works with prayer. We can pray to the saints, our fellow human beings in heaven, to ask them to intercede for us to God. One of the best saints to pray to is Jesus' mother Mary.

Write. Describe what kind of mother you would want your children to have.

Pray. In some way, pray to the Blessed Mother. Use your own words, or go to page 48 of this book and slowly read the Hail Mary, or pray the rosary.

Do. Our Lady of Guadalupe is a very important to us because she represents all oppressed peoples. She is also the patroness of Mexico and of all the Americas. Go to an Internet search engine and see what you can find out about Our Lady of Guadalupe, especially about her unusual eyes.

Write. Describe how your prayers and activities went and what you learned from them. Then write a one-sentence prayer that sums up your experiences doing this page.

Making Sexuality Honest for Your Life

The capital sin of lust means that your sexuality controls you, rather than you control yourself. In this age when so many people are hurt by intimate relationships that break up, by unwanted pregnancy, and by sexually transmitted disease, it is important that your sexuality is honest for your life. This means faithfulness for the married and abstinence for the unmarried.

Write. What is your attitude toward love and sexuality?

Pray. To Jesus' mother Mary for wisdom and strength about sexuality.

Write. Although Jesus gave us the Beatitude, "Blessed are the pure in heart, for they will see God" (Matthew 5:8), he was not talking about sexual purity. Rather he was saying that we should do things with purity of motive, for just one purpose. In other words, be nice to people just to be nice to them, not also to get something from them. How is purity of motive an issue in your life?

Do. One of the works of mercy urges us to "Comfort the sorrowful." Find someone who needs comforting, especially someone who has had relationship problems.

Write. Describe how your prayers and activities went and what you learned from them. Then write a one-sentence prayer that sums up your experience doing this page.

Praying Along with Others

Communal prayer, praying along with other people, is very important because we humans are social beings. The Mass is a way of joining with our friends once a week to celebrate that God is stronger than sin and death, and to recommit ourselves to living like Jesus.

 Write. What are some positive things about your Mass attendance? What negative aspects could you change?

Pray. Participate in a Mass or some other community prayer on a day other than your usual one.

Do. If you are not satisfied with the Liturgy at the church where you usually celebrate the Eucharist, find another place to try out. Perhaps Catholic friends at school or work might have suggestions or might even invite you to their parish churches.

Write. What is your understanding of what the Mass really means?

Becoming People-for-Others

The Eucharist is a celebration of thankfulness, especially for ways that God has brought us to new freedom. It is also a sacrificial ritual in which we offer our lives to God so God can help us become people-for-others, especially for those who suffer.

Write. On the banquet table below, draw symbols or write the names of some of the things that you are thankful for in your life. On the stone altar of sacrifice, draw symbols or write expressions of your hopes to become a better person. Include examples of people who are oppressed and suffering.

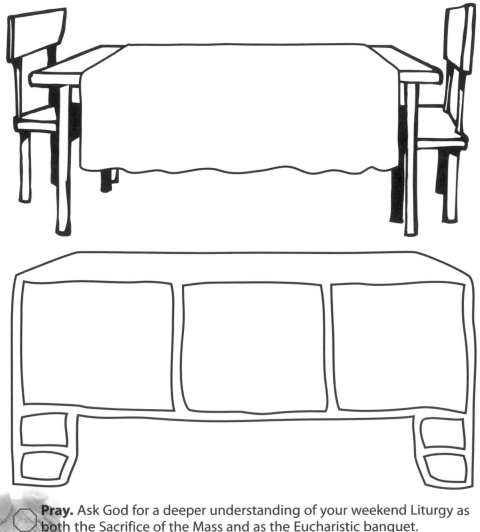

Pray. Ask God for a deeper understanding of your weekend Liturgy as both the Sacrifice of the Mass and as the Eucharistic banquet.

Radically Changing Our Lives

The themes of thankfulness and liberation, sacrifice and suffering, unite in the Jewish Passover ritual meal, the meal at which Jesus instituted the Mass/Eucharist. This communal ritual celebrates how we are freed from the slavery of sin and selfishness just as the Jewish people were freed from Egyptian slavery. It also commits us to be like Jesus and choose to be on the side of those who suffer and are oppressed, even if it means our death. We believe that with that death will come resurrection and new life. To authentically celebrate Mass means to be willing to radically change our lives.

Do. Bread and other grains like rice are the food of the poor. Jesus is bread for the world and asks us to be such bread. Bake some bread. Either use a bread machine or get someone to help you bake it from scratch. Then share it with special friends.

Do. Fasting (eating less at meals and not eating between meals) and abstinence (avoiding something—like meat, candy, or soft drinks) may seem just the opposite of a feasting meal, but we can never really celebrate the joy of food unless we have been hungry. Try a Friday of fast and abstinence to commemorate Jesus' saving us all.

Pray. Think about the deeper meaning of the Mass and pray to appreciate the Mass more.

Write. Describe how your reflections, prayers, and activities went and what you learned from them. Then write a one-sentence prayer that sums up your experience doing this page.

Inheriting the Kingdom of God

Jesus and the prophets often criticized people for their "hardness of heart." This suggests that there may be an unofficial eighth capital sin, apathy in the face of suffering.

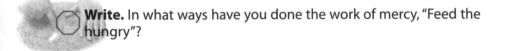

Write. Recount a time when you saw suffering and turned your face and heart away.

Write. In what ways have you done the work of mercy, "Feed the hungry"?

Write. Jesus gave us the Beatitude, "Blessed are those who are perse-cuted for righteousness' sake [justice], for theirs is the kingdom of heaven. (Matthew 5:10) When were you picked on for standing up for someone?

Pray. Imagine your death and what comes after it. What conversation will you have with God after you die? In Matthew 25: 31-46, Jesus asks people who have died whether they did the works of mercy. In your prayer, also tell God how you would like your life to change.

Do. *Final Activity*
Go to the labyrinth on the inside of the front cover. In the center of the labyrinth draw or write one thing that represents you, God, and what you got out of these prayers and activities.

Prayer Page One

The Seven Capital Sins
Pride, envy, sloth, lust, greed, intemperance, and anger.

Corporal Works of Mercy
Feed the hungry. Give drink to the thirsty. Clothe the naked. Shelter the homeless. Visit the sick. Visit the imprisoned. Bury the dead.

Spiritual Works of Mercy
Counsel the doubtful. Instruct the ignorant. Admonish the sinner. Comfort the sorrowful. Forgive all injuries. Bear wrongs patiently. Pray for the living and the dead.

The Beatitudes (Matthew 5:3-10)
Blessed are the poor in spirit, for theirs is the kingdom of heaven.
Blessed are those who mourn, for they will be comforted.
Blessed are the meek, for they will inherit the earth.
Blessed are those who hunger and thirst for righteousness,
      for they will be filled.
Blessed are the merciful, for they will receive mercy.
Blessed are the pure in heart, for they will see God.
Blessed are the peacemakers, for they will be called children of God.
Blessed are those who are persecuted for righteousness' sake,
      for theirs is the kingdom of heaven.

Psalm 23
The LORD is my shepherd, I shall not want.
      He makes me lie down in green pastures;
he leads me beside still waters;
      he restores my soul.
He leads me in right paths
      for his name's sake.
Even though I walk through the darkest valley,
      I fear no evil;
for you are with me;
      your rod and your staff—
      they comfort me.
You prepare a table before me
      in the presence of my enemies;
you anoint my head with oil;
      my cup overflows.
Surely goodness and mercy shall follow me
      all the days of my life,
and I shall dwell in the house of the LORD
      my whole life long.

Prayer Page Two

The Hail Mary
Hail Mary, full of grace,
the Lord is with you!
Blessed are you among women,
and blessed is the fruit of your womb, Jesus.
Holy Mary, Mother of God,
pray for us sinners,
now and at the hour of our death.
Amen.

Prayer of Sorrow and Recommitment
O God, I am sorry with all my heart for all my sins, for all the times I have hurt other people, myself, and You. I am sorry for these sins because of the pain they have caused others, and the pain they have caused me in my life and will cause me in my death. I am sorry that they have hurt You, my God, who is present in all people, especially the suffering. I will really try not to do these hurtful things again, to commit these unloving sins again. Please help me.

Footprints in the Sand
One night a man had a dream. He dreamed he was walking along the beach with the LORD. Across the sky flashed scenes from his life. For each scene, he noticed two sets of footprints in the sand; one belonging to him, and the other to the LORD.

When the last scene of his life flashed before him, he looked back at the footprints in the sand. He noticed that many times along the path of his life there was only one set of footprints. He also noticed that it happened at the very lowest and saddest times in his life.

This really bothered him and he questioned the LORD about it. "LORD, you said that once I decided to follow you, you'd walk with me all the way. But I have noticed that during the most troublesome times in my life, there is only one set of footprints. I don't understand why when I needed you most you would leave me."

The LORD replied, "My son, my precious child, I love you and I would never leave you. During your times of trial and suffering, when you see only one set of footprints, it was then that I carried you."